This Notebook Belongs To

Made in the USA
Columbia, SC
23 January 2021

31370455R00057